The Anatomy of Being

Shinji Moon
(Poetry from 2011 — 2013)

ISBN 978-1-300-63175-0

Cover Photograph by Shinji Moon © 2012
Internal Illustrations by Shin Yeon Moon © 2011
Shinyeonmoon.com

Manufactured in the United States of America

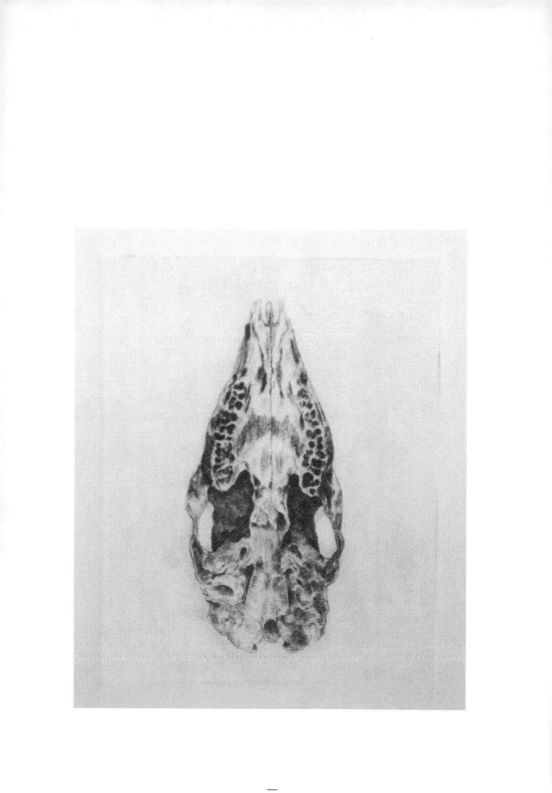

— Chapter One —

Let's begin here — at the skin. Pay attention to the story. A tale of lovers leaving port without words, with ships full of cargo, migrating from body to body, from flesh to flesh. This is a documentation of the human form: how we discover it, how we allow it to be discovered, how we love contours and knuckles and consume selfishly and sinfully — trying in vain to map out our primitive cartography without knowing what names to give the things that we love the most. This is how we discover language when we sail through it without a compass. Skin: two oceans colliding. My salt dunes. Your dimples like sand dollars. Our bodies tangled like seaweed. This is what you would find if you ran your hands over these bones in the dark and tried to turn me into braille. These are the distress signals that our body knows before we do. Morse code. Heat rising. Our skin, flushed. This is driftwood, and this is our drifting. These are my hands on your hands. These are my poems on your poems.

This is the first layer of our anatomy.
This, is our Skin.

Self Portrait

There are certain things about myself
that I romanticize, like the way I have Orion's belt on my chin
or the way my grandmother gave me her hands:
gift-wrapped and covered in flour.

Yesterday, I found a birthmark on my inner thigh
of a heart or spilt milk
and this morning I found that
there's nothing that a person can do
to make me feel more beautiful, than to
trace me like I hold
simpler lines
beneath me.

It's so easy to fool myself into believing that yes,
of *course* there are constellations on my skin, or
freckles in the night, as if my body
is a pool that reflects the sky.

But all of this
isn't me being a dreamer,
or a spilt-milk, heart-shaped romantic.

It's just me
trying to turn this husk of muscle and dirty fingernails
into something more,

as something
that I can hold like
my grandmother's hands,

as something
I can keep closer to me /
than my own flesh.

What Secrets We Keep

For so many years I've held words beneath my tongue
like I'm scared of letting them go.

Here is a collection of the white-lies, the half-truths, the
promises and the parentheses and the half-wishes on the half-
stars and the letters that I thought I had thrown out, but remained
anyways, in the back of my throat. Here is when I didn't tell you
that I loved you, and here is when I didn't tell you that I unloved
you. Here's all of it, folded neatly,

so bitter and so sweet
that my taste buds are revolting against me.

I have memorized the bones of an animal's body. I've
learned that the lower jaws of snakes unhinge so that they can keep
daring one another to eat larger and larger animals.

Sheep. Doe-eyed children. Foxes
with silver tails. A mountain lion cub: paws and whiskers
and all.

I learned how you can see the bulge of their bodies, how it can
take weeks and days for the animals to be digested, for the snake
to be just a snake once more.

But humans are told that we have faster metabolisms, that our bodies
can handle the things that we put inside of it. Everything leaves
before it hurts us too bad. Cigarettes. Meat.
Love.
Heat.

Everything, but words.

Words that
rot beneath my tongue, words that keep coming up
again like cud, that I can no longer hold onto without
my jaws unhinging — with vocabulary the size of elephants
and confessions the length of giraffe's necks breaking
every bone in my body as they resurface. Words that have broken
through every one of my teeth to find you, again, because

the truth is sinking its fangs into my tongue and
my body is begging for me to open up,

---

to let the poor
animals go unharmed.

What The Body Knows

The morning before my house was robbed, I stood at
my dresser and put all of my rings on my finger. Slowly, one-by-one,
I slid them on — my gut yelling at me to take them, to take them
all.
                                    I looked around my room as if
I knew, but I didn't — I couldn't. I only felt how my body clung to the
Doorframe, how my soul tied itself to the Mailbox, how it did not want
                                                            to leave.

When I got back that afternoon,
the first thing I noticed was that the rings were missing — that these
hands had been trying to tell me something, that my skin was a million
tiny mouths yelling *Listen*.

O, how the body knows all
          that language cannot say.

It roams, collecting signs that you're too distracted
to hear. The body is a premonition. An icicle thinks of touching your spine
and a chill run up it. Your hair stands on its toes on the nape of your
neck and you turn around to see a ghost running towards you — its mouth
          full of flames.

It turns away when it knows you shouldn't look. It watches
disasters — car crashes, hit-and-runs, the news — as warnings for your
own sake.

And as your mind
collects its poison, its milk — your body holds you in its arms.
Your sadness delivers itself into your organs.
Worry drops pebbles into your
stomach. And love —

love evaporates and condensates
onto the roof of your mouth, turning to vapor all that you
once drowned in, hiding from you all the things
that are too heavy for your soul
to hold.

Kintsugi

How often, she asked me the night before,
    Do we think it's okay to fall apart?

We live in a *break it, you pay* kind of culture.

A handle falls off of
a coffee mug and suddenly — the entire thing is useless. We learn to
sweep evidence beneath the rug, throw broken
pieces into a paper bag and never think about them again.

The Japanese knew another way. They
mended their broken vases with gold, aggrandized
the sharp corners and turned shards of broken pottery
into basins that hold light
together.

But here, there's no room for mistakes.

We give up so easily — on broken
toys, snapped piano legs, on each other — and we make believe
that even our tongues are bulletproof,
        as if we are stronger than what these
                fragile bones
                can take.

We don't forgive our broken bowls. We don't learn to
piece them back together. We trip over our own skeletons

and sweep them back beneath our skin; collect the splattering
of our sorrows and flush them down the toilet like

secrets. We're so ashamed of that which
fumbles and falls through our fingers that we forget that

there's another way: another way instead of
going through our days buying coffee at five a.m. and fucking
above the covers while rattling and spilling over, our
insides bleeding from all the damn glass.

We were never taught that
by the end of our lives, we didn't have to be made of a hundred
million cracks. We were never taught that we could have it differently, that
we could piece ourselves back together with light,
        that our bodies could burn from inside out.

Pocket Change

We walk around carrying *Closed* signs around our necks
while we press *Open* to our chests and wonder why the doorbell
never rings,

carrying secrets like pocket change
in the glove compartments of our cars that we put in parking
meters and candy dispensers, laundry machines and the little slits
between our teeth.

>   *Clink.*

Thirty minutes to love;
>   all for a quarter's price.

People change and people keep change
and we keep paying parking fines and hoping that that
means something close to love, and I'm

bankrupt from missing you, from looking for more ways to make sure
that the meter never runs to 0:00, breaking every dispenser in the
tri-state area with baseball bats to make damn sure that this never

runs out, that this doesn't have an end, as if our love
could continue onto eternity in the junkyard of broken meters,
>   as if our ribs could crumble onto each other,
>   trapping all of what we have into place.

Driftwood Bodies

Our driftwood bodies float against the tide,
twining around each other like we've been doing this
for ages, like we've been weather-kissed, floating upon
and into and onto since the time before seas were first
christened into oceans.

I touch the knots beneath the skin of your back,
trace the tree lines around your wrist,
and you smile at me and I love you
for how human you are.

Underneath the moonlight,
we laid and laughed
like run-on sentences, kissed like ellipses, and
you held me so close that I wear my bones down smooth
                                          against
                              the grain of your skin.

Cartography

I left my little black book of poetry
in the geography of your bed sheets tonight. I almost
hope you find it and see the poem that I've
written for you, or to you
on its last page.

Tectonic plates are shifting beneath my skin
and there's a new continent in my chest
that I want to call by your name.

Hazy and moonlight, you didn't know for sure
how many beats your heart had in a minute.

I counted seventy-two, but when
I ran my lips down the plateau of your
neck, it went up to
eighty-three.

The Grenade

I.

Kill me by giving me a grenade
and telling me it's your heart.

I don't want to know what your favorite color is
but I do want to know what color you bleed
when you're with me.

I had a dream that I painted my body blue
and melted into the ocean
that you swam through.

I woke up crying,
tasted salt; and thought
this is what it must feel like
to be the sea.

II.

I mean,
what else can this heart do but break or fall in love?

There's a grenade rocking back and forth in my chest
and I'm holding the pin between my teeth like an apricot pit.

My palms are mines, and you're just a finger's length away
from leaving me splattered across your chest, and you yelling "Cover!"
and pulling the sheets over our heads
won't do anything but make me hold onto you
as if you are the only thing standing between me
and a bullet.

I Never Liked Biology Before You

When I look at you laying there
across the way from me
behind the curtains of a Friday
afternoon, I wonder how it is that
you,
you are just a handful of billions of cells.

Something that I can pick apart and put back together.
You, a human with one heart
and two hands
and ten fingers
that I've fallen in love with
all at separate times.

Only that.
A handful of cells.

You,
are a textbook of our
chemistry.

Let me put your laugh in a petri dish
so that I can see if what we have
has a heartbeat,
if the cells between us
dance
like we did that evening
when you slid your arm
around the small of my waist
and kissed me
with your eyes closed.

Let me see
the way you love me
without loving me
with words.

Flash Storm

It's midnight now, and
somewhere in a November that still exists tonight
we're kissing each other's knuckles for the first time.

I've watched the juice of being in love
drip down my chin and spread like watercolors across my skin,
and I've seen what shades I feel in
when I feel in shades of you.

It's midnight now, and
somewhere in a November that still exists tonight,
we're kissing each other's knuckles for the first time.

Do you remember how raw the night seemed
when we cracked the moon over our teeth and lets its yolk
run down our throat?

Salmonella or not,
I loved you then.

It's April now,
and there are showers like they promised.

Driving around in the rain today, a friend told me
that May would be beautiful again.

But fuck it.
I don't want May flowers.

I only want
you.

Water Damage

Let me destroy everything that I've written
that doesn't have to do with the way you walk like you're trying to hold
the sky up with your palms.

I've been listening to the rain for the past couple of days, have
been listening to songs that sound like what the rain would say if she
spoke English instead of Morse code, and if my
translations are correct, all she wants is for us to stand beneath her
with our mouths open, mouthing — *kiss me.*

I love like a leaky faucet or I love like a dam breaking.
                    There is   nothing   in between.

When I met you, the little Dutch boy pulled his finger
out of my chest and suddenly, everything inside of me spilled out at once.

I puddled an ocean, rounded the corner on Third Ave all the way uptown
to Grand Central like a flash storm, and
suddenly —

I couldn't touch a thing without inflicting
water damage, without you breaking apart every molecule
that I had ever known.

Avant le Déluge

No one ever talks about what came before the flood.

Jean and Jeannette are long forgotten.
Their lovemaking wasn't stopped by the water that sloshed by their ankles.

At first, they thought it was a miracle — and underneath ten feet of ocean,
they kissed for the last time, grinning.

And when he opened his mouth to say "I love you," he swallowed
an entire sea.

The Importance of Color

Afterwards, I asked him what color he thought he was.

Skin?

No, no. I said. *Like blue, or orange, or maybe even red.*

But he didn't answer, only folded himself into sleep,
leaving me feeling as if my body were a hollow building
on fire.

Parenthetical Love

If you draw parentheses around us I'll make sure
that we have all the power of a margin note and all the beauty
of a whisper with typographic wings. I stutter and say *Olive juice*
instead of *I love you,* but does that make it any less meaningful?

I want to take long romantic walks up your arm with my lips.
I wanna picnic on the arc of your neck and sneak a bottle of wine
in a thermos with you and get stoned
somewhere on the mossy side of your ribs.

I'm wanderlust for your city and when I say
Don't take me home just yet, I really mean

*Let's share this whiskey and take a train into the city and hang our heads over
the edge of an apartment building and try to see if we can find a star lodged like a penny
in the pavement.*

The most important thing I learned from my mother
is that putting on a stamp upside-down means *I love you,*

and Look,

if it means anything at all,

I would turn over every post office in the world
just to show you how much I care.

What I Mean When I Say Touch Me

My flesh takes on other flesh in attempts to see
what colors two bodies can make.

Blue and green. Orange.
          All the colors   of volcano rain.

When my mouth forgets how to language, I sentence
with my hands.   I   curve my body like a stem .

               your eyes like open palms
                on my neck,
               knowing so well what promises skin
               can break.

I woke up in bed with an almost-stranger;   pulled myself
from the weight of his body and dropped my bones into the shower;

into the steam, and thought of how neither of us
had said anything the night before; how we
swept up broken conversations from the floors and
filled these landfills with our small talk.

                    I close my eyes.

There is a tenderness in explosions, in phosphenes spelling out *I love you*'s;
to-do lists; almost-prayers; and the dark, heavy hull of what memory
leaves behind.

I open them
and see eight million men and women walking
dreamily, dreamlessly — their eyes closed through pools of traffic;
never letting themselves be touched in ways besides what the body
has to offer.

On Astor Place, drills push themselves into concrete flesh.
Tires pull at gravel. On windy days, you can hear the subways
whistling, their catcalls snaking beneath sidewalk grates.

When I'm talking about flesh, I don't mean this flesh. I don't mean
muscles or medium rare or eight million men and women or all these
urban metaphors for fucking,

When I talk about flesh, what I mean is that I want for my words to be
touched gently,

as if you had never seen my sort of dialect before,

as if you never wanted to read anyone else
        again.

The Most Malleable Metal is Skin

I have counted the crawl spaces of the human body, have
cleared out so much of myself that when I'm quiet enough,
I can hear how a heartbeat echoes.

When you hold me, I fold into myself so tight
that you can no longer find me. Love me, and I climb the mountains
of my vertebrae to try to escape my body and touch you.

The body betrays, folding me so deep inside of itself that
I no longer feel anything when a stranger touches me into the afternoon.

My fingers are hollow shells, this skin a shroud
over what my heart is trying to tell you.

We lose ourselves in touch — in skimming and skimming
but never knowing more than what the skin chooses to tell.

But yesterday,
my heart moved for the first time in weeks. The body's little organs
fluttered enough to send missionaries up my bones and alert me
that I was blushing — that the heart was beating for someone else —

that the familiar figure who walked into the room and barely
looked me in the eye,

         was enough to make all the stones nestled in the bottom of my
stomach turn over in their seats.

In A Parallel Universe We Could've Been Something

In a world apart from this, there is a place
where we lay what the heart holds on the surface of the skin.

We are uncharted mine fields. Glass that keeps
breaking. Seven years of bad luck over and over again
until all we have is eternal damnation.

You can no longer read the news without feeling
a hundred thousand deaths like rain on your skin. You can no longer
look up without seeing the skin that the moon shed and left,
pale and waxy, in the afternoon sky.

In a world apart from this, people are even more afraid to touch.
You shake a stranger's hand and a story falls through.
You fall in love, and your cheeks bloom flower displays.

There are broken hearts scattered throughout the streets, and every night
before dawn, the sweepers come and push them all into gutters.

Here, we run our atoms together until there's an explosion of light.
Our mouths eddy together and we see what colors we can create
between us.

You are blue in flames.
I am the echo of a siren — the red
that hangs in the sky long after the music is gone.

This is a rose window we hang between us
to let the light in between our spines.

> When we first made love,
> our broken corners molded into each other
> like a mosaic.

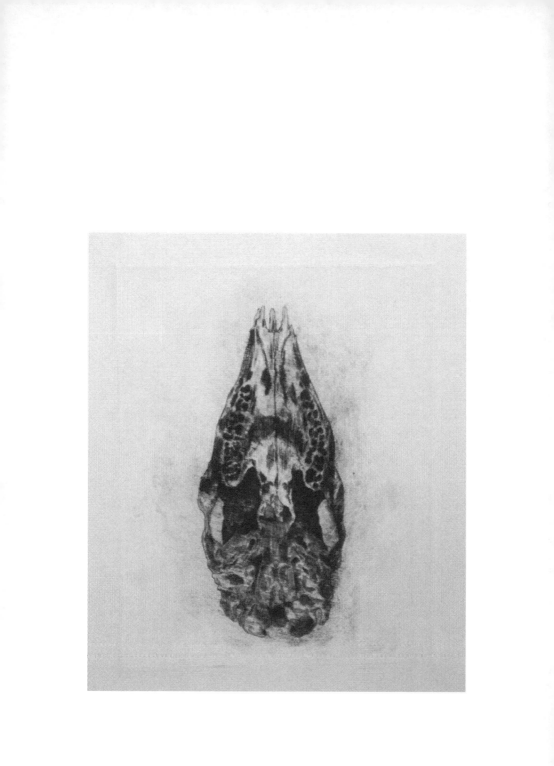

— Chapter Two —

But what happens when skin falls away? I ask my body as it peels itself slowly, skin by skin, ligament by ligament, until all I'm left with are bare bones, my stories, my arms collecting my organs and holding them close. I am afraid and my body is molting and I am afraid but what can I do? *What happens when someone touches me as more than touching me?* And my body tells me: You let them. *But what if they don't like what they see? What if the body is the only thing keeping two people tethered?* Then you learn what it means to unlove, to take yourself back from giving. When skin falls away, language takes its place. Kiss each other's margins. Fold fingers together like doggy-eared pages. Leave your boundaries behind and step out of your skin and spill in love — finally — and if love doesn't last, learn too, how to mop yourselves back up, untangle what mess the body has made, examine all that love emptied out onto the floorboards and take what was taken from you so that you don't leave in the morning with holes where he had touched you. This is the sad and beautiful song that your organs sing when you aren't looking. This is love, so close that you can rearrange each other's ribs. So close, that you can't help but leave it behind, just to see if it will remain.

Questioning Without Answering

I shouldn't ask questions that only I know the answers to, should I.
I mean, what do I expect when I ask *How did this happen?* to a boy who
doesn't know that poetry is the one thing that turns me on the most?

We're all born at the crowning of the universe and none of us ever die as
long as someone is there to pick the flowers at the edge of our gravestones
and put them in vases by the kitchen window.

> *Here is my photosynthesizing heart.*
> *It beats for you*
> *as you drink your*
> *morning coffee.*

Have you counted the freckles on your cheeks? or, do you think
seven is a humble number? — and what color would you be
if no one had told you that your skin was the shade of skin?

I hate seeing poetry in everything I touch.
I hate that I can no longer love you without turning you into a metaphor
— that it can never be simple as looking at you and saying

yes,
yes.

yes.

Because you are laying beside me, and
I press my hands against your chest and have to catch myself again

before I ask you whether or not that ticking is your heart
or the pocket watch that your grandfather had given you
all those years before you loved me.

A Love Letter to a Stranger

The first and last time I saw you, you were sitting underneath a streetlight in a cargo jacket with a hat over your eyes, reading a book about geology with your legs folded crisscross-apple-sauce in front of you, and when you smiled into the page all I wanted to do was make love to you. Or buy you coffee. I still can't tell. On Broadway in Manhattan, no one ever stops to sit and read. No one ever stops to say hello to the florist who needs it the most when the sky is as gray as it has been these past few days. Everyone's heading somewhere instead of being at the place they want to be — but you, you were sitting like a still-shot in time, with your elbows rested on your knees and a scarf looped over your neck once, twice, three times and enough times for me to fall in love. The sign in front of you had fallen, but you didn't mind because you were laughing about tectonic plates or lava rock or thinking about the first time you kissed a mountain on the lips. Around you the world pulsed. Cars shuddered. A woman with braids in her hair walked past, crying. Plates were shifting somewhere in California. Nothing had changed except you were sitting there underneath a streetlight, in a cargo jacket with a hat over your eyes, reading a book about geology. Nothing had changed but you. And my heart sputtered when it saw you and my hands shook when I reached into my purse to get the last two dollars that I had that month, and when you looked up at me a volcano erupted and covered my cheeks in a landslide of red. I asked what book you were reading and I still don't know how the words formed. Your hair was the color of sand dunes. Your eyes were springs that a girl would get naked and swim in in broad daylight. I asked you where you were going and you said *Nowhere, really* — and I thought that was the most beautiful thing I've ever heard. Nowhere, really. Nowhere, but here. There were so many questions stuck behind my teeth. Where is home? What kind of rocks do you love the most? Would you like to fall in love? But all I could say was *I hope you find what you're looking for,* and walk away, molten. The first and last time I saw you you were sitting like a small gap in the middle of an ocean. You were there and you were home. Home, wherever your skin wanted to be. I should've told you that I was going to write this poem about you. I should've told you that you could rearrange continents with that smile of yours. And I hope you find this somehow. I hope this verse runs its fingers through your hair while you lay in its lap. I hope it tells you all about the summer rain and how its first kiss felt like mist rising over the roads after a storm. I hope you kiss it square on the mouth with your eyes closed and think about your Argentine, about the woman you see when you think of every country you've ever made love in — the one who blurs all country lines. Tell this poem how you stood at the edge of the world with a beautiful someone, how you didn't know the last kiss would be the last, and how you never thought that you would spend the rest of your life looking for that same feeling in every city you ever woke up in. Tell it. Tell the world what it means to be still. Tell it, because I think you are the only one who knows for sure.

I Don't Want to be Loved, I Just Want to be Untangled.

Screw falling in love.

My heart itself is already in tangles. A web of nonsense
and a drawerful of necklace chains that I will never
have the patience to separate.

I am sounds mixed with
different mediums of light. Six thousand eight hundred
dialects of flesh that I don't have enough time to
translate into words.

I am swearing off of love because everything inside of me
is oil and vinegar and I no longer believe that it's morally correct
to fall in love with the intent of both destroying and rebuilding
another human being.

I am a forest fire and an ocean, and I will burn you just as much
as I will drown everything you have inside.

I don't want your sentimentality. Quit looking at me with the intention
of melting me. We all know it's working. We all know what this heart
is capable of unfolding.

I am not as strong as my words pretend to be. Not
as quiet as these caesuras promise. This heart is a patchwork quilt of people
that leave different shades of blue inside of me.

> The drowning. Your skies.
> A blue jay on a porcelain
> plate.

For now, I am closing off these bones for someone who will know
how to trace me without me ever telling them what I look like naked.

The love that I'm looking for falls out of the realm of your lips
and my lips and our lips doing a dance that involves bodies and more skin
and your hair touching mine, gently, like two winds
colliding.

Screw falling in love.

It's too much to handle when
I'm already having difficulties breathing and keeping track of my
heartbeats and making sure that my limbs are doing what
they need to be doing.

Because
men are so beautiful.
But this heart is so
fragile.

I am every vulnerability that the thesaurus has to
offer me and in a certain light it's impossible for me not to pull you
towards me with the intent of kissing the very life
out of you.

What I'm trying to say is that you are not allowed in.
What I'm trying to say is that all I want is to open myself up and have you
rearrange me, untangle the gold chains of my heart, love me for
every shade of blue that I have hidden in the silent spaces
between parentheses.

I have sworn off of falling in love,

        but I know that in the morning,   outside ,
        in the pale frost of February,
        all I'll want is to hold another person's hand, warm and
                    gloved,
        in their coat's pocket.

Absinthe Poem

I told a boy in London that he had eyes
that could drown a girl, and God only knows why he
kissed me a moment afterwards.

How easy it is, I thought with his hands around my waist,
to turn someone on with such a blatant desire to drown.

I stood there in the rain with a beautiful boy who knew exactly
where to put his hands and I couldn't stop thinking
of how I had never felt less beautiful.

So I closed my eyes and was there again,

to the night where we sat side-by-side with our naked bodies
in the lake, with the land and water a Rorschach symmetry;

with the stars like fish in the sky
that swam when we dipped our toes in
and made ripples, laughing, with our limbs
like broken swan wings,

and my heart caught in my throat
in the shape of your laugh.

He Loves the Rain

I think we all speak a different sort of language
than one another, but boy you sound a whole lot like coffee on a
Sunday morning. The rain falls bitter against the windowpane and
your elbows are making holes in the countertops; and I only want
to tell you that I wish I was as close as the threads of your skin, but
if I can't be that, I'll be content with drinking my drink beside you —
the rain sloppy open-mouth kissing the roof, trying to dismantle
the etymology of our conversation — our words hitting the floor like
thunder.

The First Time I Tell You I Love You

Tomorrow is the last night
till our love becomes an ellipses.
Me, leaving. You, going — the
distance between us stretching
across state lines that for me
hold oceans between them.

Please. I press my lips against your skin
like a plea. Your fingers between mine
are prayers that I've been trying to find the words for
since the first time I woke up from a dream about angels
to see you looking at me with the sky in your eyes.

Your lips are tulips in the vase of my throat.
You photosynthesize and my blood is chlorophyll.

I can no longer differentiate between your pulse and mine
and I want to tell you that *all my poems sound like sighs since I've met you*
but you're painting my neck the color of your breath
and I'm so distracted, thinking of you and your lashes
that furl and unfurl just for me, tonight.

I write those three words I never told you slowly across your skin.

Do you know how it hurts to touch you, knowing that
in the morning, I'll still wake up alone?

Tomorrow is the last night
till our love becomes an ellipses.

I don't want to think of all the suns
that will rise without you.

Greylock Mountains

A birch sits quietly a little ways away, its branches
like ribcages, white and peeling skin off of its own shoulders
against the dark fog of this molting summer.

I touch your wrist with my wrist and get them confused.
The wind turns over and your skin turns to braille
beneath my palm.

Ours is a careful verse — but this isn't
a quiet poem.

English language my ass.
When you kiss me, my syntax hits
the wall across the room and shatters
in shards of words that scatter
across the floor.

I lie against the white picket fence of your chest
and look up at a sky that's just a smudge of your iris.

I'm thinking of the anatomy of this earth; of how
the plates of your skull have hardened in such a way
that we will always be in love with one another.

The birch sits quietly
and a blue jay laughs overhead.

I say *I love you*
and the letters get caught
between the branches.

Temporary Vows

I will love you until I have nothing left to offer you.
Until the droughts come. Until my skin is nothing
but a pothole waiting for rain.

When you turn my body into a desert,
                              I will leave.

When I'm nothing but a crater holding onto your skin,
I will peel myself off of you as if leaving is the same thing as
molting, and
                    in the morning, you won't remember my name.

              Only a shadow. Only the window open, a light on, a draft
                              coming in from beneath the door.

Looking For Atlantis

There was a night when I was younger
where I fell in love with Atlantis and swam
a thousand leagues beneath the sea with stones
in my pockets to get to a place
that I wanted to call home.

                                    You are asleep,
and this is a confession as much as it is a fairytale.

I can see the moon like a silver spoon through your window
and your body is curved like you're fitting yourself into the crow's nest
of our ship.

I left the warmth of your weight because I dreamt again of a night
I want so bad to forget, and I'm sitting here with my heart on the edge
of this seat, feeling like I'm peeling my limbs off of a sidewalk.

There is a drought and there is a drowning,
and tonight — your arm
is a lifesaver around my
waist.

"What Should We Dream of Tonight?"

— You and me in Greece. It's beautiful out. We're laying beneath an apple tree and everything is slow and tepid. It's summer. It's so warm. There's an apple tree and grapes are vining through the fence.

— No, come on. We can't dream of something we're doing already. We can't dream of just laying here.

— Okay. So we're in Greece, still. But we're in the water now. The water so blue, so blue that we can taste the color. And we're swimming and we've been swimming for hours and it's all so clear that we can see the entire world beneath it. So, we're swimming. We're swimming forever. Did I tell you I always dream of swimming? Swimming and sharks, too. I dream of sharks a lot. So we're swimming, but for the first time there's no sharks. Did you know that whales have hearts big enough that they can fit a child in their aorta?

— So, did we see a whale?

— Yeah. We saw a whale. A beautiful humpback whale. It combed us through its teeth and it tickled. Like this.

— Ah! Stop that. No tickles.

— Alright. Wait, don't kiss me I'm telling you a story. Anyway, the whale combed us through its teeth and we landed in a chamber of its heart. And inside of it, there was a map. It was a treasure map. We were so happy when we found it, and we thanked the whale and swam out and followed the map's trail on the back of a sea turtle until we got to where we were supposed to be.

— And where was that?

— Ah, Atlantis. We found Atlantis. And it wasn't the Atlantis that they told us about in stories. It was dark and it was terrifying and it seemed like it was haunted by ghosts. It was grey. Think Manhattan, after it had been abandoned for a hundred years. It was awful, and we couldn't understand why it was so. But Neptune found us, with his crown still faintly gold. We asked him what had happened to his city and he said that it was taken over by the darkness, that the light had left. People had stopped believing in it. Neptune wasn't the place that it was since the Kraken stole the pearls away. And, we told him that we would help. Your idea. And he told us of the four mother of pearls that kept the entire city glowing — but how since they were taken, the city fell to disrepair.

— The kraken did it?

— Yes. The kraken. We went to his home in a crevice, just a tear in the ocean floor. And while it wasn't looking we took the pearl from it. It was almost easy. A little too easy. And, um. Oh. You're distracting me. Do you see the lights outside?

— They're grey. It's night, Shin.

— Yes, but also a little red and a little blue. Anyways, three of the pearls were easy to find. The kraken had flung them in various stretches of the ocean, but we were fast swimmers and we had all the time in the world. Another one our whale friend found for us. He had held it in his aorta for years. It had given me grief for he didn't know what it was, where it was, till Neptune sent out the signal that he was looking for the light once more. We found another in a forest of seaweed. And the fourth pearl, that one was hard to find. The last pearl was rumored to be up on land, in a museum somewhere in Manhattan. A pearl so big that had surfaced on the Hudson River and had scientists so amazed that they had trapped it in glass as a showcase. The humans had turned it into a spectacle. As usual. And we had to get it back because Atlantis was getting darker and no one seemed to know but us. It was hard but we took it back. I won't go into details because you were there, you know? But we took it back. We had to steal it. They wouldn't understand if we asked. They would've thought we were crazy, maybe suicidal, if we told them we had to bring the pearl back to Atlantis. But we took it back, and we lugged it in a net back to Atlantis, and gave Neptune back all the pearls. And slowly, light flushed through the city again. The darkness drew away like tar, and what was left was the light that we had been looking for for all of our life.

After a certain point, it was time for us to go back up to land. We had to go back because we can't just leave the world to hide away, to escape. So we said goodbye to our Atlantis friends. Neptune gave us the treasure that had brought us there in the first place. But, this was the kind of treasure that we liked. It was full of historical documents and beautiful little things — mementos of people's lives. Old watches. *The Heart of the Ocean.* An old book. Sentimental treasures. We took them back home up to land, back to our grimy cities, back to our homes, back to all of the hurt and the sadness and the darkness that we couldn't fight away with pearls. And we realized that we were unhappy. And suddenly, we understood why Atlantis chose to sink.

So, we went back. We packed up a small suitcase. We could save Atlantis but we couldn't save our world, our cities. Everything here was grey and the people wouldn't stop hurting each other and every place reminded me of how I had hurt you. I had hurt you up here. We both felt it, but we couldn't say it. And one day, we couldn't take it anymore and we returned. We went back to Atlantis because there, we knew nothing but the light, but the love, but each other. We went back there because we couldn't hurt in a place protected from the darkness. Down there, we knew nothing but floating, but swimming. There, there was only light. And it was beautiful, how we loved each other — the way that we lived, for all of eternity, down there, where nothing could find us, where the world no longer mattered.

—

—

— I love you.

—

—

— The end.

Wicks

Remember our summer nights.
        The polyester diner seats.

How the low glow of our love for each other lit every candle
around us.

How we never had any lighters. How we never
thought to bring matches.

But how we burned anyways — as if we were
born from gasoline, as if we were molded out of
                                      flint.

The Interpretation of Dreams

"I love you more than ever," you tell me while my professor lectures
on dreams. *Form,* he says. *Context,* he says. There is a table
and then there is what we make of it. There is a house
and then there is the home where mother cries
without peeling onions.

"I love you more than ever," you say, and I pull myself
between the words and weave myself so tight that they can't slip away.

Displacement, the professor says, and I'm already
in the second row, dropping my heart into a beaker of water
and watching the weight of it spill out over the edges.

This is how much
the heart weighs.   This is
                    how much of you I can translate into flesh.

Last night I dreamt in and out of buzzing, of pollen, of being caught
in a windowsill — my wings burning from the light.

I pressed two stars together, swallowed the pulp
that it left behind — and folded away my wings for winter.

"I love you more than ever," you said — and I peeled the
words apart until all I saw were the hollows of hives.

"I love you more than ever," you say, and I
drip honey into my mouth until I'm full.

A Rendition of Autumn

There was a point in our lives
where if I slit my throat, it was you who would bleed.

We say goodbye too often in Autumn.
Tonight, the last leaf fell off the tree beyond my bedroom window
and I could hear the sound of branches aching for love to wrap
around their leaves like limbs.

It was three a.m. in the last stretch of May.
Springtime calls for heartbeat symphonies
and when we pressed our bodies together they coincided like
chords,

like staccatos when I ran my hand down your spine.

Fog is one of the top reasons that drivers get killed each other.
In the backseat of my car we almost caused
the hundredth casualty,
but all I got were bruises in the shape of apologies
along my thighs.

There are certain people who leave scars when they go.

Tonight I cut my thumb while peeling an apple.
I thought of you.

Expiration Date

The sell-by date on today's milk carton is the
same one I see behind my eyelids.

Time curdles everything it touches,
                                        doesn't it?

The cut on my thumb is shaped like my last love's smile.

Verdict: History repeats itself, sometimes in ways you
                      wouldn't imagine.

There's redemption in the night sky tonight. I whisper *Forgive me*
to no one in particular, and the clouds tiptoe away silently.

I'm writing you a letter that I'll burn over the stove
just to watch the light between us flame and burn out again.

When you left, you took my words away.

Now, when I think of you, all I'm left with
are paper cuts where your hands used to be.

Fragmented

A star slits its throat on the moon tonight,
bled over its white basin and watched the color drain from its skin.

My English teacher calls those who read poetry sensitive,
so maybe it's not my fault that the smallest things break me,
not my fault that even my blood cells are cracking like
glass.

My words have become fractures as of late;
splintered bones, dark skeletons of lost poems and journeys home
from places where love sinks beneath the floorboards.

I can't concentrate on these letters, on the way that
I'm supposed to draw out *I love you*'s into five hundred character stationary.
I can only look at your nouns and say verbs. I can only look at your skin
and see coordinates for a place I'd like to call ours.

Because there's nothing more honest than loving in fragments,
than cuts in the riverbank and the broken bottles that wash up
as sea glass beaches. There's nothing more to it than the way
a lover can interject a kiss by telling you that you're beautiful,

        or the way my skin is paused by tree lines, the way
my fingertips spread out like deltas into flesh-toned seas.

Last night, the moon was a bloodied red and today, I painted my lips
the same color. On my way home at one in the morning I was cut off
by a passerby and change scattered between us like broken
words.

                When I looked into her eyes,
I saw two full moons that she had stolen from streetlights.

            Everything
            is getting muddied these days.

        Streetlights in eyes and verbs in place of nouns.
Words are broken mechanisms and I keep leaning on language
as a weak-ankled crutch.

And with pen against page, I still hear my blood cells cracking,
breaking ; and

49

with each comma, I
                          fracture.

Social Hemophilia

Let's call it social hemophilia.
Someone touches me and I bleed for days.

There's still a photograph of the two of us
somewhere in Manhattan.

I think of that often,
more so than I think of you.

It's like this. Autumns have always harbored the loneliest people
and the loneliest people have always found harbor in me.

I can no longer read old journals after I'm done writing them
because there are certain things that bleed
long after they've been stitched up and
tucked away, but on nights like these — when my reflection
is a stranger with my haircut,
the only words that comfort me are my own.

Dear Diary,
I can't remember the last poem I read before he kissed me
and that makes me sadder than it should.

Dear Diary,
My hands shake when I think of his hands shaking
and I'm sorry if my existence is a run-on sentence but
I have no time for semi-colons and caesuras when
I'm trying to stop myself from bleeding out of these lines.

And again. Dear Diary,
Today I met a boy whose hands I wanted to crack open
and put my own between.
What the hell do I do now?

This Is What Distance Does

We measure catastrophes by how close they hit to home.

There was a shooting at an elementary school
an hour from my home. When I heard, all I got were chills
and a slow wave of sympathy, but the grief of thinking of
the first-sized heart of my brother lodged
twenty-six bullets in my chest.

There was a hurricane in New York City.

In the darkness, we ran down the streets laughing,
terrified, our bodies wringing themselves into beads of sweat,
the water hitting our cheeks like ice.

No one from home called
to ask if I was alright.

To them, the storm was just a little rain.

I couldn't tell how much I hurt you from
two hundred miles away, couldn't tell how bad you wanted to
wring my throat from so far
away.

The Richter scale will tell you how difficult it is
for you to regain your footing after an earthquake.

I am so sorry for not being close enough to feel your body's
vibrations against mine.

> I'm so sorry for not being brave enough
>> to brace our storm.

The Conversation Between the Bird and the Hand

Why do you always leave?

Won't you will always be there with your hands outstretched, waiting for me to come home?

But what if I must leave too?

But I love you.

But what if I must leave, first?

But I will starve.

But what if I find another bird?

The loneliness would kill me.

Then why don't you stay?

Because I have only ever known the sky, and you are so beautiful that touching you hurts, knowing that one day — you may die and leave me here, with only this blue: with only this endless, endless blue.

If I Left You A Voicemail This Would Be It

I almost miss the sound of your voice but know that the rain
outside my window will suffice for tonight.

I'm not drunk yet, but we haven't spoken in months
and I wanted to tell you that someone threw a bouquet of roses
in a corner trash bin and I wanted to cry
because, because — well
you know exactly why.

And, I guess I'm calling because only you understand
how that would break my heart.

I'm running out of things to say.
I've stopped stealing pages out of poetry books, but
last week I pocketed a thesaurus and looked for synonyms for you
and could only find rain
and more rain
and a thunderstorm that sounded like glass, like crystal, an orchestra.

I wanted to tell you that I'm not afraid of being moved anymore;
not afraid of this heart packing up its things and flying transcontinental
with only a coat and a folded-up address in my pocket.

I've saved up enough money to disappear.
                    I know you never thought the day would come.

Do you remember when we said goodbye and promised that
it was only for then? It's been years since I last saw you, years
since we have last spoken.

Sometimes, it gets quiet enough that I can hear cicadas rubbing
their thighs against each other's.

I've forgotten almost everything about you already, except that
your skin was soft, like the belly of a peach, and
how you would laugh,
making fun of me for the way I pronounce almonds
like I'm falling in love
for the first time.

The *Water Cycle*

Falling in love with you was a kind of melting, and
falling out of love with you wasn't at all like rebuilding
ice cubes out of fog, but rather
evaporation, condensation, and then the rain
once more.

My heartbeat keeps me awake at night
and I don't understand what language it speaks in so
I put a stethoscope to my chest and plug it into my laptop,
but Google Translate still hasn't found
how to turn water into words,
or an ocean into a novel
about the back of a whale's throat.

The heart
is never as simple as a one-liner.

The heart
is a burning shipwreck under four thousand layers of sea.

What I've come here to do tonight is this —
salvage what I can from the wreckage
so that I can rise again, like a phoenix, into my own skin.

I touch you, and my heart undergoes the water cycle.

Evaporation and condensation, and then
always,

this rain.

The History of Water

This is the history of water: how it drips through faucets
and touches our skin,

> how the monsoon season floods the Han River
> every summer and swallows one of Seoul's bridges
> whole.

Every meniscus holds a thousand hands, holds Death and Birth and
whatever may come in between. It remembers how we swam naked
with our bodies made of sixty percent water, the small islands
of our skin surfacing, barely   touching.

We stand naked in the skeleton of my shower, history
pooling sudsy around our ankles — with our skin like oil against the
rain — holding ourselves together as dewdrops collect on the foliage
outside of our windows back home. We kiss, and our mouths collect
sin and miracles, faith and piss — four hundred wars
cleaning the dark hoops beneath our eyes.

We wash each other clean with the dark bones of
secrets, of loss, of famine and fall and friends like us who became
lovers by accident, as

> magnolia suds collect like salt dunes by our toes; Our
feet pressing against the sand, the tide cleaning but never
forgetting,

Water repeating itself again and again, our ghosts clogging up
every drainpipe in this city.

Shipwreck

Salvage what is left by creating a model of a shipwreck
and putting red flags over all the things you hate about the way I love
like a sea urchin, with my spine on the outside and the soft,

soft hull of my chest curled inward like I'm protecting myself from
you, or you — from me.

A hundred years from now, someone will find us.

They'll sift through the remnants of the night we last saw each other.
They'll pick apart the things we left behind before we fled
our skins. There, the letters. In the closet, a pile of clothes that I
never wore.

The photographs. Some, blurry. Others,
smears of ocean. There is the portrait of you sleeping. The
small rings that I left behind every time
I left without really leaving.

There are our skeletons — our bones wrapped up and jumbled
into each other so much so that the excavators won't be able to tell
whose belonged to who.

Your humerus against my femur. Your hipbones against my
kneecaps. Your phalanges wrapped around my thighs.

Salvage what is left by pulling sea glass out from your palms
and showing me what bloody consequences come from trying to send
messages meant to shatter out to sea.

I'm holding myself like a wounded crow between my own hands and
I have flown a hundred miles to get to a place where the
language no longer has words for forgiveness.

You were a dialect I was once so fluent in. You were the first
word that I wanted to write.

A hundred years from now, someone will find us.

       You,   sitting like a stone on my chest;

                  my bones broken in half to make way for the weight
                         of all that you've left behind.

The Haunting

This is our echo.
I put my ear against the wall and hear the moans
from the last time your hips pulled their tides against my shore.

Our movements reverberate and we mistaken them
for a home shifting in its seat.

A priest once told me of the phenomena created by your own
energy trapped like heat in the walls around you,

                    how you create your own poltergeists
from slammed doors and those hours you spend beneath your
bed sheets, trying to smother your own lungs.

When you wake up in the morning with bruises around your neck
and no one to blame but yourself —

Leave.

This is a wounded home; our bones have been
cracking themselves in halves and quarters for years and years
and years enough for secrets to collect in the crawl spaces.

I found a black and white photograph of a young boy. Of
my grandmother, standing at the kitchen counter,
chopping radishes as big as her grief, her hands
covered in flour.

I am ten years old somewhere in these walls.
In my old bedroom I lay on my childhood blanket
and feel the soft, cluttered breath of a child who held too
many broken things inside of her.

This is the window where I fell in love with a man
years older than myself.

This is the stain that the moonlight made
that afternoon we couldn't say *I don't love you anymore.*

This is how we cater to our ghosts:
by taking them inside of us;
by letting them become the volume of our lungs.

For Something I Know Too Well To Name

How often it is that we turn each other
into metaphors, months into men, this summer a summer
that belongs to us and us alone.

And you, had we not been in love that May
all those years ago, would the post office still equate a
secret, would a yellow taxi still mean leaving, and would
a train platform still make me cry when dusk hit sin Manhattan?

Mark Doty's partner died of AIDS and everything Doty has seen since
has looked like loss. Sylvia Plath killed herself and afterwards people
could only approach ovens and apologies with remorse.

The flowers in our common room keep dying. The
fruit in the bowl is always barely there.

How many times do we say goodbye before we leave? How
many times do we pretend that absence can leave us fuller than before?

Once, I believed in you like a poem, turned your heart
into a metaphor for my heart, turned our months into honey
and caramel lozenges.

But metaphors come and metaphors go, and
not even seasons
                        have the courtesy to stay till dawn.

Instruction Manual

Maybe it'd be easier if we all came with an instruction manual
to show us when it's appropriate to cry in front of someone else.
I need an oil change every five years or else my heart stops ticking
on time. A kiss on the neck means self-destruct. Trace my back
and I'll start hydroplaning.

Thumb through this how-to-pamphlet on how to keep your fingers from
shaking when you're sitting beside a boy who can say your name just right,
and let me know what page I should go to when I want to know
how to survive this winter without burning all these matches
just to relight my own eyes.

How do you keep the monsters at bay? Check page 67.
How do you cook a Thanksgiving turkey without dropping it on the
floor and making your mother cry? Turn to page 18.

What number do I call
if someone replaced my bones with broken glass?, because
I don't think insurance covers that.

I'm an old model. A 1994 edition of a car that
                              you probably didn't want in the first place.

This radio doesn't have all the stations and
the glove compartment doesn't even have
any gloves in it, but I can promise you
                    at least this:

     I will never fail to inflate my lungs for you when you're
              a hundred miles deep,
              heading headfirst
                    towards a telephone pole,

     —   screaming   —

       because you have pulled out all your own
                                   brakes.

Nocturne No. 1

I.

The cars outside your window
are slurring their tires against the asphalt
like a bar encounter with his hand
too high up her thigh.

It's somewhere between twilight and our night
and for now, I'd rather stay here, in the low lamp's glow,
with one foot beneath the sheets, and you,
so close to me,
       the warm honey of our love a blanket around our shoulders.

I tell you that the world outside the window
is too loud for my hands to take in, and your nocturnes
touch my nerves shyly. You
play one of our songs on the guitar and I kiss you
so you lose the notes like pennies between the couch cushions
of my lips.

I write your name and my name
with a heart around us in
the margins of your sheet music.

                        Sometimes,
I fall more in love with an echo than the real thing.

II.

My name has more syllables than the *'sea,'* but tonight,
I'm not nearly enough molecules to be larger than its blue.

Hold me like a sound ricocheting inside your bones.
Hold me, smaller still.

How can we touch each other and not disappear?

All I want is to be a note, played softly by your palms —

— with you,
unrolling me softly,

my skin as blank sheet music
whispering *pianissimo.*

Nocturne No. 2

I.

This is the dream again.
You are on me like a hundred different drops of rain.
I am naked and you've slit my spine down the middle
so my soul stops sneezing from all of the dust.

II.

Tonight is a holy kiss and every dreamer is a priest.
My religion is in skin and poetry and making love with my eyes
closed under the moonlight, but I still sit in churches
and pray when someone I once held hands with dies
during the night.

III.

Some of our wishes are making the sky throw up stars into empty craters.

IV.

The moon
is nothing but a hundred moths about to take flight.

When they're gone, oceans will sink. Atlantis will rise
and their people will tell us, laughing, of the great parties that we've missed,
how *Davey Jones is a fucking riot!,* and how the anglerfish
line the walls every evening to set the mood for midnight.

V.

My favorite thing to do is drink with you until we're both
crawling up each other's limbs to see if we can reach the skyline.

The night is a hundred different kinds of light.
The sun rises, and my soul burrows underneath your skin
until the moths spill white dust over our palms
once more.

What Goodbye Means

The winter was so cold that you could peel whole islands out of the sea.
Even the animals started skinning each other for warmth.

The aftertaste of a Goodbye is the worst to get rid of. It's a warm, brown
        sugar that melts softly into
                brine.

There is no finality in words, no period at the end of every sentence.
We are ellipses, caesuras, the pauses between blinks   and the
                                        breath ,
            is the most important part.

What end does a goodbye offer when even our echoes
can cause avalanches?

There is a well in our hearts and every night
the water freezes over until I can no longer think of anything but lost
language, lodged in the iceberg of my mouth.

Everything is still here. The letters I wrote are still stuck
between my teeth. My old home still has my name scratched
on the underside of my windowsill.

And still,
your mouth on my mouth
is a thought as fresh as
melting icicles away
with my breath.

— Chapter Three —

Absence is what I found when I left my flesh behind. The grief is present in the bone marrow, as muscle loss, as your joints being able to tell when the rain comes, even before you. Loss is so apparent in our anatomy that we have given the space between our ribs a name: *Intercostal.* Once, I had tried to fill myself. I plastered caulk over my emptiness. I filled my body with cement. Rubber glue. Love letters. Broken things. I tried to fill the emptiness with those which that only had holes in them, and everywhere I went — things fell away, toppled out from behind me. My negative space became a prison.

> *Does absence have flesh?* I asked my body.
> *Only the one you created,* it said in return.

Fill Me

It's so sad to feel you've been
drained of your yolk,
hung upside down by your ankles
with a hole poked in your chest,
while a man with blue, maybe gray, maybe the land in his eyes

smiles at you
as every color you bleed
seeps into the floorboards, seeps
through the apartment linoleum,
through the air vents,
and underneath that eggshell carpet,

while the family underneath
looks up at their ceiling as
mother pulls out her phone
to call the plumber.

Because this is not the first time
this has happened,

and her living room is stacked high
with bowls and pots that slosh
every time a human cries
for the last time.

Self-Defibrillation

Writing these poems hurts in all the places it shouldn't.

Please.
Don't pick at your scabs to see if you can find a story underneath.
Red continents line your knees and all our stories begin the same,
with, *I was drunk and fell on the sidewalk, cracked open my skin
and bled a memoir.*

Leave those stones unturned.
Save them for another poor soul who doesn't know
that living in this world means killing yourself to prove that you're
a phoenix, rising.

Because it's one a.m. now and I'm coughing a bloody poem
into tissue paper. With my head over the toilet bowl I'm choking out
regurgitated aches. I feel my heart beating through my fingernails
and by three a.m. I'll have given myself open heart surgery
by the glow of the computer screen.

                    This poem is
                    self-defibrillation.

        I can save myself
        just fine.

It Took Time

This is a poem about
how you never get the kiss you want
when you want it;

how time twines around your neck, its thorns
digging into your skin so you can never forget
how clinging to a string of hope, threading it
between your spine, and having it unravel before you
in the span of an hour
is worse than any metaphor about nakedness
that you poets will ever write.

This is my reflection in the mirror. This stanza
is the small gap where my fingers try to touch against
the glass.

You can't even possess yourself; let alone the person
you see standing before you.

                    The moon
hasn't come back from the cleaners yet
and I have nothing to slip into tonight that makes my reflection feel
beautiful.

Time is falling through the holes in my pocket. January
is coming soon, and I have a feeling he's never going to fall
out of love with December.

He'll still write her love letters. He'll send her
white orchids on every lonely holiday and pretend that love
is a place that you can cross state lines to get back to,

but it's that time of the year again, and
calendar sales keep reminding us all that we can never get back
to where we once wanted so bad to lose ourselves in
for good.

A Physician's Handbook

I write *"and for the first time"* so often that often it's all a lie.
Words have meanings that try to explain that which
cannot be explained; like the emptiness of having once, and never
having again; the sadness of turning over one night and smelling
someone you love like a poltergeist on your bed sheets.

Your body aches. You can feel yourself sighing all the way to your knees.

        Now tell me: what is the word
                                 for that.

This is a physician's guide to the human body.
Your femur is called something else entirely with my eyes closed.
You slip your phalanges underneath my vertebrae and all of a sudden
this poem is making you sweat.

Sometimes, you wake up as a dark spot on the sun,
and you can't tell how you get so burnt.

The man who accused me of stealing the can of soup that I stole
apologized for doing so.

I guess I deserve that I can no longer fall asleep in this city
without seeing his round and humble face,

                      the name tag on his uniform,

and the way he still watches me as I walk through the aisles,
waiting for me to look up at him and wave,
        his palm raised in apology.

Miscommunication

It's evening now and I sit thinking of diners
and *please comes* that I should've responded to.
A phone call the other night ended with smoke on each line
and a voice telling me that I would never know what it meant to love.

Then silence — a dial tone — and a quiet
walk in the night, wondering if everyone knew me
better than I know myself.

This is a poem about a lot of things, but mostly it's a poem about
how words get lost so easily between two — how
stories can be built out of nothing, filling the space
between a last kiss and today's nothing
like an eighth sea.

A boy once read a poem of mine and saw his own silhouette in it,
thinking that I was referring to his eyes,
his lips,
to the way he touched me
                — just so —

but really it was about a boy whose name I never knew
who left a flower *'to the girl in the blue dress'* on my hotel doorstep,
who I loved simply, because he came
without a story, because he knew nothing of
mine.

There are days where the sky is porcelain and we hold it
between our lips to take a sip. Pale days.   Stale days.
The coffee is cold and the neighbor has the mower on again.

There are so many things I want to say tonight,
of all nights,

but I don't know where
to begin any longer.

Merry Christmas

Good god, what I would give
for another body next to mine tonight.

I couldn't tell you which is more difficult —
this physical loneliness or this draft that I feel between my heart valves
like I left a window open somewhere in the third story of my soul,
a candle blowing in and out, swaying
with each of my breaths.

Remember when we sat dockside with our feet hanging over the edge
like we were fishing hooks trying to catch love
around our ankles?

We were quiet so that we wouldn't scare it away,
and how when I cup my palms to my ears, I heard the sound
of the Atlantic, and suddenly
winter became that much harder to bear.

Things tend to get to me so easily these days.

Winters have always been the loneliest days. When I look up
past the window I can see the north star, but I'm not sure
if it's guiding me home or leaving me
behind.

I sliced my finger open on a can of cranberry sauce because I was
thinking of how love never finds me
when I long so bad to leave my skin for good.

My hands don't know why they're touching you as if
I could give my life to you, and this well inside of me has frozen over
and I'm so cold, trying to figure out how to
burn, once more, as I had done in the
summer, as I had done
when you loved me.

I Used Poetry as an Excuse for Sleeping With Someone Else

I no longer deserve to read beautiful poems
when nothing inside of me is a mirror of the truth. I speak, and
a hundred lies fall through.

I spent eighteen years digging myself holes to fall into, and now
I can't lay across my bed without detonating all these damn mines
that I had spent years setting down.

How often is it three a.m. with you feeling
like you're standing beneath a landslide with your mouth wide open?

I'm underneath a mountain of things that I can never take back, and
facts are the only things these days strong enough
to break me.

The stone I threw through my garage window when I was eleven
was real.   How I told my father it was one of the neighborhood
                  boys, was not.

And you,
when I told you I loved you I meant it.

When another boy fucked me in the bed
where we had made love, all I wanted to do was
leave my body there for good.

I am a carcass of regrets and apologies and things
that always go wrong before they never become
right.

The left side of my brain is where I keep
all the things that I should have said in the first place, and
these little apologies that I carry around like marbles
in my head are more true to me than what I have
done.

The fact is this: I broke your heart. Black and white, I
am the one at fault. But there is an ocean of colors that I cannot
show you, an ocean of reasons why I needed to hurt you so that I could
hurt myself in return.

There is so much inside of me that I have built up
from air. Carbon dioxide lies. Carbon monoxide truth.

But the one thing I know for sure is that I would gladly give
it all away — if it meant you would

                                      love me
                                      once more.

This Is No Longer About You

For more than I wanted to admit, you were the one
that I wanted to feel the earth rotate with.

Your black hair on my black hair was black enough
to create a hole for us to lose ourselves in.

We were two bodies pressed against each other but not
reaching in. Surface skimming skin on skin; one hand behind my
back with my fingers crossed. My heart in my back pocket
where I knew you wouldn't find it.

We were two bodies pressed against each other but we were
still separate by 360 degrees.

There have been so many sunsets that my fingers are running out of
fingers to count on.

This is the first time you see your new friend cry. This is how
you hold her, your hand on her knee, your eyes trying to melt
into a color of deep apology.

I'm sorry that the world always takes and never gives.
I'm sorry that each day dies just to give birth to ne that you already knew.

A boy with black hair and black eyes and a sharp jawline
fucked me in the bed that we made love in.

I'm only digging holes
for myself to fall into.

Little Accidents

Last night at a dive bar
my friend reached for my hand and I mistook him
for some man that I had known months before.

What is the name for a person who can't keep her hands straight?
I mix up palms and forefingers and callouses until I don't even remember
the shape of my own wrists anymore.

I stopped to buy a bottle of wine on the way back to my sister's apartment
and saw two boys my age with bloody necks and a third with
broken bottles between his hands.

A girl in a push-up bra lunged at them, screaming for them to

    fight,

                        fight

      fight.

Before I could be pulled away, I stepped closer
and touched the wrist of a boy with bloody skin, and

when he looked at me, I saw in his eyes
the world,
as it burned.

What It Took To Understand

In the passenger seat of your car, I ask you what
color the burnt orange of the leather seats are and you tell me
burnt orange. My cheeks in the rearview mirror are the color
of burning, and when I look down at my hands, they're so pale
that I forget for a moment that I own flesh over these bones.

The fog is so thick that I could lose you in it again, you say —
and I put my hand on your hand until I mix our fingers up.

There is a shipwreck between your ribs and it took eighteen years
for me to understand your kind of drowning.

The divorce papers say Christmas and July. That's all you were given
to touch the cheeks of your small daughters and try to tell them in
smaller and smaller words how absence does not mean
leaving.

The first and last time I saw my parents together was in a
parking lot at McDonalds. They didn't speak to each other, didn't
look each other in the eye — only handed me between them
like an insult.

When I got into my father's car, he handed me a Happy Meal toy
like an apology.

There are people who cannot be held quietly. There are screams
that are never externalized. If I looked at the photo albums of your
past twenty years, all I would find are decibel meter graphs of
phone calls and the intensity of your silence as you sat
smoking cigarettes in the garage.

Absence doesn't make the heart grow fonder, scientists have finally proven.
All it does is make you that much more aware of how many
feet it takes to walk a mile.

There is a shipwreck between your ribs. You are a box with
fragile written on it, and so many people have not handled you
with care.

And for the first time, I understand that I will never know
how to apologize for being
one of them.

Describing the Color Blue

There were smudged skies on the night my stepfather had a stroke.

We peeled off our clothes and jumped with our skin on into the lake water.
The sky above us was a pale stomach and our chests were small islands,
surfacing. I laid there with my breath in my ears, not being able to
differentiate between floating and sinking. The dusk was not so beautiful as
it was an eerie blue — a sunset without a sun, a day translucent enough
that you could see its veins underneath. Our small, naked bodies in the
harsh and unforgiving light. Blue lips. Goosebumps. A nakedness so
innocent and so rare; honest in its purity. There was nothing to hide and
nothing to tell, and the water trembled where we touched it.

Quietly, we felt as the world swayed beneath us.

One, two three. One
two three.

Driving home, we listened to the Beatles softly with the windows down.
Through the rearview mirror, I could see you with your heads hanging out
— letting the wind blow straight through your skins. Eyes closed. Your
bodies summer damp in this world that wasn't our world. The night was a
ghost in the passenger seat: so there that it couldn't even count as a dream.

— Chapter Four —

When the archaeologists found the remains of her underneath the rubble — they didn't know, at first, what to think. There was nothing left: no skin, no flesh, no muscles or bones or marrow. Everything had unraveled years ago — but what was left was a small light, so strangely familiar that they knew it was human — as if a soul had been bound and knotted in a small space between pebbles and stones. They held it, felt its quiet warmth. Its pleasant small of rain: its petrichor. How it beat, softly — as if for them. And they didn't show anyone what they had found — only hid it in their pockets, knowing that they had found some human truth too fragile for the world to understand just yet. *Hope,* they wanted to call it. *Love,* they chose not to say. *The soul,* they mused over drinks that evening, their loose tongues saying what they were too afraid to say in the day. And for once, they had no questions. They only sat by its light as it burned, laughing together, their faces illuminated by its light. And when they woke in the morning, it was missing — but all of them felt, as if by some strange turn of fate, as if their skin had been scrubbed in their sleep, as if their eyes — looking outwards, were finally looking, instead of simply seeing. And all of them, as they would later report, felt, if not hope, as if their souls had spilled out into the rest of their body — as if for once, they knew what all of it meant.

Let There Be Light

and God saw the light was good, / and he separated light from darkness.
He called the light day, and the darkness night. / So evening came, and the
morning came; / it was the first day." (Genesis 1.1)

Tell me how you dreamt of charming bees and woke up with a swollen tongue. Tell me about resistance, about how it felt to slam your flesh against doorframes to try and create Coltrane blues out of your skin. Tell me about the first time you lost your innocence and just how good it felt to lay with the devil between your thighs. How you cried. How you picked yourself up afterwards, your body churning — and how you walked around afterwards as if you were wearing your skin on backwards. Tell me, because underneath that light there is a darkness. There are spots in your thoughts that the sun doesn't hit. Tell me about your chiaroscuro. Your light. My dark. My dark and your light.

This is the dream of a room. An apartment. A city with a balcony with day and night hanging with their bodies pressed together outside the window. There is your skin on my skin on a skin of white bed sheets and my black hair flooding the page and bleeding all over reality. There's this flood, the way we keep falling into margins with black font. There are broken bottles from the night before that I walk over in the morning, as if I couldn't feel glass spines snapping beneath me, as if it didn't remind me of how we used to drive around for hours, drunk in the back of strangers' cars — throwing bottles out the window and laughing all the way. There is a God, or so they say. And he tells us, *Let there be light* — and suddenly you are smiling and your tongue is burning my lips so much that my entire body is well-done. That man in his dark room turns our globe on its axis and suddenly, my thoughts are sunburnt. There is a small child picking up flowers from the pavement and tucking its petals in his coat pocket. And like fate, the blind men see. And suddenly, a village falls deaf.

There was a time where darks and lights eddied together — a time where you and I weren't pulled away from each other and even oil and vinegar were in love. There was a time, but God said, *Let there be light* — and so it is that there is a you, and so it is that there is a me. God said, *Let there be light* — and the businessmen learned how to clock in on time.

So tell me again how you were a child catching fireflies in glass jars, only to have forgotten to poke the holes in the lid. Tell me about the way the light falls across your floorboards at two thirty in the afternoon; how panic sets in when you wake up in the middle of the night, the moon tracing you over like a crime scene. Of chiaroscuro. How one night, you woke up, with the light falling over your cheek — with the darkness creeping over from the other side.

Advice From Dionysus

Burn all your bridges
just so that you can build them again
with thicker ropes.

Hurt all the people you love
and then commit every felony to win them back.

Drown yourself in bleach until not even Heaven's light
can compare to how bright you burn.

Turn yourself inside out
and paint your organs the color of what you see
in your dreams.

This is the art of
living with a ticket heart — a grenade you
throw through windows to make a
point that language
has no room for.

This is how I destroyed you. And this, is how
I kept you alive.

Dig yourself a ditch, six
feet deep, and bury everything that you've ever
said, everything that you've never
meant, and everything that has
burned you and left you with nothing
but what's
left.

Chasing Sunsets, Led Zeppelin Playing

The gold-toothed guard wouldn't let us drive through the cemetery, so we chased the sunset another way — through the brushes of civilization, the thickets of 117 — we skidded tires across the asphalt so that we could bleed into the bleeding, too. Sometimes it's okay to cross over the hills in hopes to get somewhere more beautiful. The sun sets in the West and tonight that's the only direction our compasses know.

How may times can I write love songs for these in-betweens? The muddy place between day and night, the muddy place between you and I, the way I watch as you hold in the fresh air between lighting up cigarettes and turn to me, smile, and say: *Sometimes the best thing is that breath,* and how it all turns back to how we did this once before, twice before, a hundred times before when we were seventeen — how we drove down the roads almost in love, looking at each other over stop lights and laughing because of the air, of the breath, of the two of us close for the first time in months, the love between us never waning but always growing, filling in the distance between my New York and your Paris — our music burning holes into the atmosphere.

Officer, when you ask for my address how can I tell you that the golden light of a winter skyline hits the ice across these ankles so beautifully that I no longer remember what home means? The rearview is a framed photograph of everywhere that I once was and will never look back to be. The same roads are always different whenever I come home, but Sofie, with you it's always all the same. Here, is where I always want to be — talking about love, talking about what it means to be young and what it means to be happy and how grateful we are for our sadness. We look at how we have grown, how we can measure it in days, in weeks, in months since we've last seen each other — and I hold your hand and keep smiling because sometimes this life only makes sense when we're together.

This is where I was born — on the road between two families, between my mother and my father, between two wrongs that almost make a right, in the place where you can reach only with sirens and the north star and driving into the sunset into the dusk into the night, burning through tanks of gas just so that we can be somewhere where no one can find us. This is it. We're chasing the sunset with the windows down, our voices carrying across the sides of highways disobeying every speed law that you ever thought to enforce upon us.

This, this is it.
This is what they always told us never find.

A Thousand Paper Cranes

for S, who is 3624 miles away

I would fold
a thousand paper cranes
for you,

would fight away all those demons
that leave scratches over your skin
just so you know
that they don't leave through
bloody trails.

I look at you and see all the ways
a soul can bruise, and I wish
I could sink my hands into your flesh
and light lanterns along your spine
so you know that there's nothing
but light
when I see you.

Listen.

When the wind blows
all your candles out, when the stars
turn to plumes of smoke,
when your mother makes you watch
as the matches burn out in her eyes,

Let me hold your hand, your skin,
the stones you've swallowed in your sleep.

Let me
slip your soul out of your skin
so you can sleep in my palms
for tonight.

Hope In Sedona, Nevada

Hope do you find strength?
— **Anonymous**

You are what my sister saw when she stood
looking across the mountainscape of Sedona, Nevada.

When she came home she brought souvenir stories: tales of
medicine men and shamans, of prayer circles and
how a man asked her what she saw when she looked at
the raw land, and how

She had said: *Hope.*

Hope, in the silhouette of those white-peaked shifting plates,
she had found you — said your name — made you real, in their
eyes. And he told her that what she saw in those mountains
was what decorated her own bones.

And it's true.

It's summer now. The milk dew of our home keeps leaking into my
lungs. My father keeps talking of moving, and every day the smell of
wet paint reminds me that we are always leaving, always
coming, always
                              somewhere in between.

But *Hope,* do you hear me?
I've been meaning to call you for days now, about the way
I've forgotten how to screw my hands on right in the morning, or
about the puddles I leave in my wake, or how sometimes
even looking out the window is enough to make me
weep, and I think you've given me the wrong number, but

Hope? I think I found you. I think I found you the last time
I toppled into myself so hard that my knees rubbed against my
chest plate like I was a cricket who lost its meter, and

Hope, I want you to know that I believe in you like I believe
in the soft heart of my sister, who tumbled the glass of our childhood
in her palms so that I would never have to tread on anything but
a sea glass world, and

Hope? I want you to know that I'm here. With these
thin wrists and gawky words and screwed on too-big too-small limbs,

I am here.
With every ounce of my fist-sized heart.

Because Hope, you have come and gone for so long as if
my body is a revolving door, and

I have realized for the first time that I don't need to
look for you anymore. Because the medicine man told my sister
that she had Hope inside of her and,

Hope? I don't need your strength
anymore.

Because this morning, I stood on my roof
as the sun chiseled its way into every single pore of my
body, and I realized that I am

made of flames, that if you touch me,
you will burn — that I am the only match I need

to burn.

This Is What My Mother Taught Me

This is how you take oil paints off of your hands
with turpentine. How you baste a turkey — how you dance to make
all the men fall in love with you.

This is where you put your hands, Shinji — you,
who are so uncertain of what limbs are made for.

The things you've inherited from me are all the characteristics of an ox.
Drive forward. There is nothing
to be afraid of.

Your friends are insane. You have your grandfather's
nose. You are loud-mouthed and stubborn, and there are few men
who will be capable of tolerating that kind of
presence.

But, you are beautiful. Look at how you've grown, my darling. My
clementine — my sweet, sweet peach. You are a garden that comes to me
only every other season, and I have watched you grow without me,
but into me — so much so my skin.

Before my brother died, my hands couldn't stop shaking. When I
found out, I understood that the body itself is a premonition.

Fate, my darling, is something very powerful.

The man you end up with doesn't have to be tall or dark or
handsome. Look at El Rodo. His fading orange hair. His age.

Now look again, at how beautiful he is.

There is a difference between having sex and making love,
and this is something very important for you to understand.

You will always be my little girl and
sometimes, your choices will break my heart.

There is a lost childhood between us,
and no amount of time together can replace the fact that another
woman braided your hair in the mornings in my place.

I've saved both of my wedding dresses for you.
Look, I've even got your flower girl shoes.

Tone down your damn lipstick, and listen to all the warnings
that your soul gives you.

Because Shinji, you don't know everything. And one day,
you'll know even less.

And honey,
you are still the same little girl who sat down in the middle
of the dance floor and threw petals all over
the white reception, crying — and that, that is
nothing to be ashamed of.

This Is What My Father Has Taught Me

Let me teach you about the Ottoman
Empire, how dynasties have fallen and risen again and
again, how you never appreciate cities until they have been
earth-struck windswept / with
all their secrets blowing at hundreds of miles an
hour, cutting your skin with all the sharpness of corners
and papers, tool sheds and broken love that they haven't
learned to let go. Forgive me. It has taken me
so long to forget. / Blood is always thicker than
water and you come from two such powerful blood
lines, so what are you running from?
Keep your priorities in order. Eat heartily. Eat
healthily. Remember that I love you. That I miss you.
That I llama you.
You can move people with your language.
I'm sorry that I found out in a way that hurt you.
Schoolwork comes first. But your health is more
important. I can tell when you have stayed up all night
smoking cigarettes out your bedroom window
/ covering up the scent with incense . / You are not a child
anymore, but you will always be my smallest drop of
love. It's okay to listen to the sad songs you listen to.
But you are too young to be full of so much of the world.
You have your mother's something. You have something of me in
you. But I can't say for sure how you have happened — you,
with your hands full of Earth and your head full of
rainfall. How many hearts do you hold in your own?
Remember that you can only have
one. Anything more would kill you. Anything less would
drive you to where I am now. Don't let the pain of the
world entire you. Don't look at me for
an example. I only have answers. I only have broken language
to show you where you should go. When you stop asking questions, there
is no more hope. Don't forget where you have come from.
Don't forget where you have once called home. I will always
be here for you, even when you betray me — even when you
leave me for something more. You are my kin. My daughter.
You are the child that I did not want but only have
love for now. I have taught you all that I didn't know I could
teach you. I have spent eighteen years of my life for you
but that doesn't mean you owe me anything except for love. Except
something. Except a future where I know you will be okay.
I am a minister for your dreams. I will help you sow them into reality.

Hold my hand. My pinky with your palm. You are a small child in a big
girl's clothes. You are so much and I know that you will break my heart
but I am learning now that that's okay. That
I have broken yours, too. That history repeats itself, sometimes in
ways that you wouldn't imagine.

A Letter To My Own Daughter at 18

When you want to fall — fall.
Evaporate and condensate,
but when you rain, come down
as a hurricane.

If the birds stop chirping, if the sunlight forgets
you, if you've got your shirttail caught in the fence
of your spine, and you have no way of getting
loose,

remember that I am here, that I will bail you out of
your own prison, that I will lay with you the morning after
you fall in love and tell you that it's okay,
that it's okay to trust another human being
with more than you knew you could.

I will tell you how I held you as a child, listened
to your heartbeat on those sleepless nights, that I
loved your small body and your pebble fists and blessed
the skeleton inside of you —

that you are not beautiful because
a boy tells you so, but beautiful because
you exist.

And I apologize for giving you such nervous hands and
a sine wave heartbeat. And when you start putting question marks
after everything you say — know that

I may not always have the answers, but
together, we can try to make sense
of it all.

I'll take you back to my West Virginia. My Gloucester. My
honeysuckles and tool sheds. The chicken coops. The abandoned
loves. I'll show you what the August grass feels like. I'll
distract you with tree roots, with atlases, with lessons about the
sea, and until your question marks are bent into
arrows, I will not

stop. So shoot them blindly. Hurt and be hurt. Be the bird
as much as you are the hand.

For I will stand behind you, breaking every vow that I made

to protect you. When I notice your wings are peeking out
from beneath your shirt collar, I'll

tie my hands back from clipping them. I will hide every rope
in the country so that the love inside of me doesn't
tether your ankles to home.

You are eighteen, and you are free.

But when you want to come home, I'll be here.
In the wind chimes, in the small moths that flutter
towards your light, in the way dawn still breaks the same
blue eggs in every place that you decide to
go,

I'll be here.
Less a ghost than the wind.
Less the wind than a soft hum in the back of your
throat, telling you that it's okay to sing, that it's
okay to bray,

that your song is a song that you'll spend
the rest of your life trying to understand.

That when the birds talk you into flying south, it's okay
to pick up
and leave.

Here is What Our Parents Never Taught Us:

You will stay up on your rooftop until sunlight peels away the husk of the moon,
chain-smoking cigarettes and reading Baudelaire, and
you will learn that you only ever want to fall in love with someone
who will stay up and watch the sun rise with you.

You will fall in love with train rides and sooner or later you will
realize that nowhere seems like home anymore.

A woman will kiss you and you'll think her lips are two petals
rubbing against your own.

You will not tell anyone that you liked it.
It's okay.

It's beautiful to love humans in a world where love is a metaphor for lust.

You can leave if you want, with only your skin as a carry-on.
All you need is a twenty in your pocket and a bus ticket.
All you need is someone on the other end of the map, thinking about the supple
curves of your body, to guide you to a home that stretches out for miles
and miles on end.

You will lie to everyone you love.
They will love you anyways.

And one day, you'll wake up and realize that you are too big for your own skin.

Molt.
Don't be afraid.

Your body is a house where the shutters blow in and out
against the windowpane.

You are a hurricane-prone area.
The glass will break through often.

But it's okay; I promise.

Remember,
a stranger once told you that the breeze here is something
worth writing poems about.

Here Is What I Wish They Said

There's a world beyond this world that you need to tune into. Pick up the universe like a radio signal. Fall in love with white noise. Inspire and be inspired and realize that it's only human to love so many at once. Love yourself. It's something that took me a long time to learn, but it's one of the most important things that no one has ever taught me but myself. Forget about the weight that you need to lose and the way your skin doesn't yet fit your bones the way you want them to. Don't let your body dictate what your heart is made out of. Let the world in and sooner or later people will see the oceans pouring out of you. You'll walk down the street and someone will mistake you for the sky. You are beautiful because you let yourself feel, and that is a brave thing indeed. Treasure the company of being alone. Think of solitude as another friend for you to hold hands with in the dark. You shouldn't be afraid when even the night is too afraid to chase its own tail. You have clipped wings and scars from when people told you that you were too young and too human and too weak to try to scale the troposphere with your eyes closed, but you were born from the earth and you were born from a wave of your mother's love and you will end up somewhere in a horizon between the two. A nine year old girl wrote me a letter for Christmas and said, *I don't know you, but I was told you were beautiful and kind and wonderful and I don't doubt it for a second.'* When was the last time you wrote a letter to a stranger? Love those you've never seen. The intangibilities are the reasons why I fall in love so easily in the first place. Touch people without your hands and they'll remember you longer than if you found them with your fingers on their leg one night at a dive bar. Give yourself up to carnal pleasures and taste the ripe fruit of being eighteen and in love with the promise of goodbyes, but remember that you are always looking for someone that you can say *Hello, hello, hello* to without ever worrying about the front door shutting behind them for the last time. Love and be loved. Everyone is human. Hold your aunt in your arms while she cries on your front lawn. Don't let your father go out to watch the movie he wanted to see with you, alone. Everything goes back to how much you see, how much you feel, how you lasso your heartstrings around others. Look out. There is a world outside your window where wind chimes know your name better than you do. Fall in love so often that you can't tell where you last left your heart. Let me hold you in my mouth and make love to your senses. Remember: you are only human. Remember: you are not the skin that you were born into, but something tenfold, a thousand leagues deeper than that.

— Acknowledgements —

A thank you to the friends I've made on Tumblr.
Thank you for supporting me, for giving me such kind words, and for allowing me a space to grow.

To my English teachers throughout the years, thank you for believing in me. Appa, for allowing me my dream and for supporting me every step of the way. To Shinny, for the beautiful illustrations and for being there for every little bit of my life. To my Mom because you both once told me to follow my heart no matter what, and since then I've been living so much happier. And to Mitsuyo Sasaki, for teaching me how to love.

Collin Leitch, for being there with me from the start. Alex Bernstein and Meggie Royer, for editing my first manuscripts and giving me the most thorough critiques I could ask for. To Aran Armutlu, because we're in this together. To everyone who has touched me and inspired me to see the world in a more beautiful light. To Sofie Manetta, Nick Scaglione, Nicole Shimer, Natalie Lagnese, Jenna DiMicco, and Grace Wolff. Thank you. And to the people who inspired so many of these poems — rock on. I couldn't have done this without you guys.

From the bottom of my little heart, thank you.

Thank you all.

" Why do you write poetry? "

Because I have forgotten everything else.
Because there are questions that no one has answered. Because there are
dreams that have snuck up from behind me and left burns in the places
that I can't reach with just my hands, with just my skin. Because there are
muscles that I've only just discovered the uses for. Because there is no
other place for me to go but here, a place where there are only more
questions — only more metaphors, only more excuses. Because I'm scared
of cutting into myself with a knife, and have found that this page is an
incision, that these words are sharper than the blades that people have dug
into their stomachs. Because there is light just as much as there is darkness;
because the man who works in the falafel truck on Third Ave no longer
knows my name. Because there is such a thing as love. Because there is no
such thing as love. Because I have only just reacquainted myself with my
parents — have seen them as humans instead of holes. I write because I
am finally giving in to my own name, am no longer running from where I
have come from and am no longer running towards anything and because
the only place where I can feel myself feel is in paper. Because margins are
no longer cutting it for me. Because I have forgotten my first two
languages. Because dialect. Because words. Because there are gaps between
teeth and gaps between people and people still wonder why there is such a
thing as loneliness. Because there are dead that don't want to rest. Because
there are living that want to be dead. Because my Writing teacher told me
that my favorite author was an asshole. Because I'm trying to prove that I
exist, that I'm alive, that I'm not a mistake but something blooming.
Because I saw a dandelion blooming between sidewalks. Because there is
still no cure for sorrow. Because skin. Because I can no longer look at the
world without metaphors. Because there is no answer. Because there is no
skin. Because there is no vessel but this. Because this book is yours as
much as it is mine. Because I keep answering questions with more
questions, and there are question marks between myself and other people
and I can no longer keep myself from wondering why that must always be
so. Because I have seen love — have witness loved, have touched love,
have fought with love, have tried to drown love only to see it again one
morning, making me coffee in the kitchen — humming a song that I
thought I had forgotten. Because there are people that I'm scared to call.
Because when I think of voicemails I think of bad news. Because my
stepfather had a stroke. Because my father is a different man. Because I
have lived so many lies. Because my grandfathers were great men. Because
there is a world that I will never see. Because you broke my heart. Because
I broke yours. Because we still don't understand how that could be so.
Because. Because. Because I still love you. Because I always will. Because
you are the most honest verse that I have ever never written. Because fuck
poetry. Because fuck me. Because please. Because yes. Because you.
Because this.

Shinji Moon is a student at NYU in the College of Arts and Sciences. *The Anatomy of Being* is her first book. She's received awards from her hometown's *Young Writers Award,* as well as from Scholastic Arts & Writing. She believes that poetry is the only way to get people to hear her, and so far — that has proven to be true. She wants to learn how to say *You're wonderful* in every language, and so far she has gotten to Finnish. *Olet ihana.* She currently resides in the city with notoriously delicious bagels, and the other night — she dreamt that she found Atlantis. But in reality, it was just an old washed-up bottle.